Axolotl

A Complete Pet Owner's Guide

Axolotl care, tanks, habitat, diet, buying,
life span, food, cost, breeding, regeneration,
health, medical research, fun facts, and
more all included.

By: Lolly Brown

Foreword

The first time you gaze at an axolotl through the glass of a tank, you may not be sure what you're seeing. Clearly, it's not a fish.

For one thing, this strange aquatic creature has legs. On either side of the head there are three sets of plumy gill structures that resemble feathers. Dark, lidless eyes peer out at you above a mouth that seems to be smiling.

You're looking at a salamander, *Ambystoma mexicanum*. Sometimes called the Mexican Walking Fish, these amphibians are closely related to Tiger Salamanders. They come in many colors, but all trace their origins to two freshwater lakes in Mexico, Xochimilco and Chalco.

The axolotl has survived since the days of the Aztecs. The lakes have not. All that is left of Xochimilco today are canals in and around Mexico City that are increasingly threatened and polluted by the ongoing growth of that thriving metropolis.

In the wild, the small remaining axolotl population not only suffers the consequences of pollution, but also the presence of intentionally introduced competitive species, in particular, non-native tilapia.

The axolotl is on the CITES endangered species list as a result, and is now rarely seen in the wild and depends entirely on the efforts of conservationists for its few safe havens.

The axolotl survives in captivity, however, due to its popularity as an exotic pet and for its importance to the scientific community.

Huge numbers of axolotl are bred in captivity each year, and the creatures play a crucial role in the study of wound healing, trauma, disease, and aging due to their uncanny ability to rejuvenate lost limbs and even portions of their brain and spine.

The axolotl retains its juvenile morphology throughout life, and is completely aquatic. For the hobbyist, an axolotl has a high interest value balanced against its relatively low maintenance needs.

They are placid and easily trained, quite willing to eat out of your hand and capable of recognizing their owners.

There is something undeniably whimsical and charming about an axolotl crossing the tank to greet you when you walk into the room. They often put a paw on the glass in greeting, and, while perhaps not a "cuddly" pet, the species is surprisingly interactive.

In forum discussions, enthusiasts talk about how their axolotl follows their motions and routine by walking around the tank and watching. The creatures enjoy attention, and will even sit upright to catch your eye and initiate interaction.

It is a misconception that an axolotl simply sits in its tank and does nothing. They are fascinating creatures that quickly engender the affection of their humans, making this unusual salamander a favorite among the many choices of exotic pets suitable for life in an aquarium.

Acknowledgements

I would like to express my gratitude towards my family, friends, and colleagues for their kind co-operation and encouragement which helped me in completion of this book.

I would like to express my special gratitude and thanks to my loving husband for his patience, understanding, and support.

My thanks and appreciations also go to my colleagues and people who have willingly helped me out with their abilities.

Additional thanks to my children, whose love and care for our family pets inspired me to write this book.

Table of Contents

Table of Contents

Table of Contents

Table of Contents

Table of Contents

Table of Contents

Chapter 1 - What is an Axolotl?

The axolotl is an amphibious salamander (Ambystoma mexicanum), indigenous to Mexico. Sometimes called a "water monster" or Mexican Walking Fish, its name is derived from the Aztec language Nahuatl. The closest translation in English is "water dog."

These unique creatures were once considered to be a culinary delicacy. They are mole salamanders, and are among the most primitive of their kind, diverging from other salamanders in their development more than 140 million years ago. This fact is only the first in a long list of items that make the axolotl a truly unique creature.

Chapter 1 - What is an Axolotl?

The first specimens appeared in Europe in 1863. Today, axolotls are rarely caught in the wild and are listed as a CITES endangered species.

Axolotls are, however, widely bred in captivity for their value in medical research involving limb regeneration, trauma, and anti-aging. Additionally, the large size of the species' embryos makes them useful in a broad range of disease-related studies.

Hobbyists find the axolotl an intriguing choice among the many aquatic creatures that can be successfully housed in an aquarium. While fully-grown axolotls will live peacefully with one another, they can exhibit cannibalism when they are younger.

The axolotl is a fully aquatic species. They cannot survive out of water, and they are neotenous, meaning they remain in their larval form for life.

Axolotls are Neotenous

The reasons for the axolotl's neotenous state are not clear. It may be a result of the species development in waters with insufficient stores of iodine.

This would compromise the presence of the hormone thyroxine in the salamander's body and keep it permanently in its larval state.

Another theory suggests that water temperature may prevent the thyroxine from functioning appropriately. Some experts even believe the axolotl de-evolved to a fully aquatic state because they were safer in the water than on land, a theory that extends to other species that naturally live in bodies of water at high elevations.

The axolotl has gills and fins, with only rudimentary lungs. The gills are, in fact, one of its most prominent features, rising in feathered pairs on either side of the salamander's head. Technically called "rami," the gills are full of capillaries or "fimbrea."

As a neotenous life form, the axolotl is regarded as a backward step in evolutionary terms. It is thought to be an offshoot of the Tiger Salamander, a species with which the axolotl can breed successfully. (For more information about the Tiger Salamander, See Appendix 1).

If an axolotl is treated with hormones, it will metamorphose, but this rarely happens spontaneously. Claims by enthusiasts online that they have a creature that has done so are almost always a case of mistaken identity with a Tiger Salamander.

Physical Characteristics of the Axolotl

An adult axolotl measures 7-14 inches (18-35 cm). They are poikilothermic, meaning that their body temperature is completely dependent on their surroundings.

Temperature is, in fact, highly important in their care. They do not tolerate temperature fluctuations and need colder water than tropical fish.

Feathered Gills and Breathing

Their prominent and feather-like gills are highly functional breathing systems. The gills pull water through their membranous structure so the capillaries can extract oxygen from the liquid and feed it into the body.

In turn, the gills also pass waste carbon monoxide back into the water. The axolotl does not need to move for its gills to function. The structures move or wave gently on their own to perform their oxygen-gathering function.

The gills are obviously very fragile, but even if they are harmed, the salamander can still breathe quite well. The gills grow back quickly, and the axolotl actually has "back up" breathing systems.

Other Forms of Respiration

In addition to the use of its gills, axolotls are capable of cutaneous respiration. When the salamander moves, or when the water itself moves, oxygen passes through the creature's thin skin and into its body.

Too much motion in the water, however, will stress an axolotl to the point of death.

Finally, axolotls also use buccal respiration via a flap at the back of the throat, the buccopharyngeal membrane. When water passes over the structure, oxygen is extracted. The same membrane functions to allow the axolotl to suck water into its mouth for feeding.

Although not sufficient to sustain breathing for long, the axolotl does have very primitive lungs. They can "sip" air at the surface, but more times than not, this does little more than cause them to swallow a bubble and float until they manage to burp!

(If an axolotl goes to the surface repeatedly to gulp air, something is chemically wrong with the composition of the water in the tank. The likely culprit is a build-up of toxic ammonia.)

Distinguishing Gender

It is extremely difficult to tell the difference between a male and female axolotl, which can lead to a lot of surprise births in captivity.

Any time that you choose to house two axolotls together, most anything can happen, so don't be surprised if you find eggs in the aquarium.

Determining Sexual Maturity

At full sexual maturity, females appear rounder at the end of their bodies, while males are more elongated, with longer tails and a larger cloacal region, but often only an expert can make this distinction.

If the vent (the area behind the back legs and under the tail) is examined closely, both genders have a small bump that is actually a cloacal gland. In males, the bump is much larger.

In white, golden, and albino axolotls you can tell the animals are fully mature if their toes are dark brown, and the soles of their feet appear to be dirty. Other color types may have darker toe tips, but it's more difficult to see.

Young axolotls will develop to adulthood in 18 months to two years. If well cared for, they can easily live to 15 years of age.

Color Variations and Types

There are no different types or sub-species of axolotl. Do not let breeders suggest otherwise when you are shopping for a pet.

These are highly specialized creatures indigenous only to the area around Mexico City, which largely explains the perils they face in the wild. Part of their unique nature lies in the fact that they have changed very little in their evolutionary history.

The spread of Mexico City has all but erased the axolotl's native habitat and placed the creatures on the CITES endangered species list.

Although conservationists are laboring to create safe havens for them, the axolotl's ultimate fate in the wild is highly questionable.

Chapter 1 - What is an Axolotl?

Known color variations of axolotl include:

- gray,
- various shades of brown,
- golden albino,
- black,
- cream,
- and piebald.

Wild specimens are the darkest in color.

Each type has a specific name, and often axolotls are sold according to this designation. The names do not, however, denote different species of axolotl. There is only the one type.

"Wild" or Brown Shades

The brown shades are the most common seen in axolotls, ranging from a warm tan to near black.

It is common for the body to exhibit some spotting or speckling and frequently the belly of the salamander is lighter than the back. In sexually mature adults, the toes often become pale.

This variety is, however, the most surrealistic looking, and is not as popular among enthusiasts who prefer more dramatic color variations.

Chapter 1 - What is an Axolotl?

Albino and Golden Albino

Any animal that is termed an albino lacks skin pigmentation and therefore appears to be white. Albino axolotls, however, can range from cream to yellow, and the body may seem to be shaded.

The real telltale sign of albinism, however, is the presence of red eyes. When albinos reach adulthood, their feet and toes are grayer in coloration.

Golden Albinos have a lovely, warm tone that can almost seem to glow. Like their paler cousins, however, they have the same red or bright pink eyes.

Typically albino axolotls have really beautiful gills that are pink or red, in striking contrast to the pale tone of their bodies. For this reason, their look is even more exotic. Arguably, these are among the most attractive members of this species, and highly popular as pets.

Melanoid

Axolotls termed "melanoid" do not display the typical shiny areas or "iridophores" generally seen on the body and around the eyes of this species.

These specimens are almost jet black, but often with a paler underside and toes, especially as adults.

Chapter 1 - What is an Axolotl?

Leucistic

This color variation is easily concerned with the albino axolotl. The skin is very light, but a leucistic axolotl's skin does contain pigment, and can be speckled with black. When this occurs, the creature is said to be a "piebald."

Also, a leucistic will not have red eyes, and their eyes are generally encircled with a black ring. They are also highly popular as pets because they sport the same pink gills as an albino, if in somewhat more muted shades.

Copper

Copper axolotls are most commonly found in Australia, where the species is the only non-native salamander that may be kept as a pet. The color is very much like caramel in most individuals, but can be much darker.

These axolotls also have red eyes, but that fact is often missed due to the color of the creature's skin. The gills will be the same color as the salamander's body.

Axolotl Biology

Because axolotls are completely aquatic even though they are amphibians, they cannot leave the water to colonize new habitats.

Chapter 1 - What is an Axolotl?

Basic Axolotl Anatomy

Eye

Front Leg

Gills

Dorsal crest on back extends down along the tail.

Rear Leg

Tail

Adults are 7-14 inches (18-35 cm).

In an odd twist of fate, the fact that they have been cultivated for medical research has saved the axolotl from sure extinction. Now, in addition to their value as a lab animal, they are increasingly prized as exotic pets.

Although a carnivore, the axolotl has only pedicalate teeth that look like little cone-shaped stumps. The teeth can be used to grip food and to move it around in the mouth before swallowing, but the meal goes down whole.

Chapter 1 - What is an Axolotl?

Even if your axolotl should nip at you, the bite won't hurt. The little guy just doesn't have the equipment to do any damage.

Like all amphibians, the axolotl has a three-chambered heart and, as mentioned, rudimentary lungs. This is not, however, a typical feature of their kind.

The vast bulk of amphibians can live in the water or on land. Axolotls, however, will die if kept out of their aquatic habitat for too long.

Regenerative Abilities

These salamanders are famous for their ability to regenerate their limbs within a few weeks. Any damaged appendage will form a bud from which a new foot or leg develops. It is even possible for an axolotl to regrow portions of its spine and brain.

Occasionally, this regenerative ability goes awry, and a perfectly healthy axolotl with four functional legs will suddenly grow a fifth appendage. This is nothing to worry about, and could be a consequence of the degree to which axolotls have been inbred in captivity.

As long as the axolotl is able to function normally, and can feed, it doesn't matter how many limbs it does or does not have. If, however, an additional growth or appendage is causing the salamander to suffer, the advice of a veterinarian should be sought.

Chapter 1 - What is an Axolotl?

Although no one likes to contemplate intentional cruelty, it must be emphasized that you should never inflict any kind of damage to your axolotl, no matter how minor, for the purposes of witnessing their regenerative powers.

Young axolotl heal very quickly, and are often able to replace a lost or damaged limb within a month. Older animals may require several months. The process is not effortless by any means, and becomes more and more difficult as the salamander ages.

Chapter 1 - What is an Axolotl?

Chapter 2 – Keeping Pet Axolotls

Bringing any pet into your life is a commitment – or should be. Sadly, many creatures that live in aquariums are often considered to be "throw away" or worse, "flushable" pets.

Axolotls are intelligent, long-lived creatures. While they are not especially demanding, they do require – and deserve – appropriate care.

Consider each of the following points BEFORE you bring an axolotl into your life. Be honest with yourself about the answers. Keeping a carnivorous, aquatic pet like an axolotl is not the best option for everyone.

If you cannot deal with the realities of axolotl ownership, be kind to the creature and to yourself and abandon the idea.

Never acquire any kind of companion animal only to decide in a few short weeks that you've made a mistake.

In a case like this, "buyer's remorse" can have tragic consequences.

What to Know Before You Buy

Above all else, do not get an axolotl as an impulse buy. What seemed like a good idea in the pet store may seem like the great-granddaddy of all bad choices within 24 hours.

For one thing, the tank in which the creature will live should be aged for at least two weeks to create appropriate water conditions before the salamander is placed inside.

Beyond that crucial fact, think about the following before buying.

Long Lifespan

The most important thing to know before you buy an axolotl is that they can live 15 years in captivity, with 8-10 being the recognized average.

If you are not willing to commit to the creature's care for that length of time, don't get one!

Chapter 2 – Keeping Pet Axolotls

Completely Aquatic

The axolotl is completely aquatic. You can interact with the salamander in the tank, mainly through hand feedings, but you can't take it out and pet it. That being said, you may be surprised when you realize your axolotl recognizes you and greets you when you come in the room.

Subject to Stresses

Don't simply assume that because a creature lives in water that it cannot show affection, or that it is unaware of life on the other side of the glass. In fact, an axolotl can be too aware of what's going on in your world.

Stress is a major source of death among these pet salamanders, which may mean they are not a good choice for a child's pet. Certainly a young child will not be able to handle the tank maintenance chores alone.

Questionable as a Child's Pet

Young children must be made to understand that they cannot bang on the aquarium glass nor do anything intentionally to frighten the axolotl or elicit a reaction. These creatures will sicken and die if they are unduly stressed.

Plainly put, for all their charm and personality, an axolotl may just be too boring for some children. Gauge the personality of the child in question and weigh your options for appropriate pets.

If a high-level of physical interactivity is a requirement, the axolotl isn't a good choice.

Axolotls and Other Pets

Other animals can also be sources of stress. It doesn't matter if the family cat can't get at the axolotl. If Fluffy spends all her time on the other side of the glass staring at the poor salamander, or worse yet, pawing at the aquarium, the axolotl is still going to be scared.

Also, tank mates are not an option with the predatory and carnivorous axolotl. Anything else in the tank that moves is fair game and will likely end of being lunch for your salamander.

Don't make the mistake of thinking you can introduce an axolotl into an existing tank. Remember, these are freshwater creatures indigenous to land-locked mountain lakes. They need water that is cooler than that used for tropical fish.

Sensitive to Blockages

It is also imperative that nothing be introduced into the axolotl's environment that is smaller than the creature's head. To eat its food, an axolotl simply opens its mouth and vacuums in whatever is nearby.

Anything the salamander can't digest is a potential digestive blockage waiting to happen.

This also means that you can't use normal aquarium gravel. The salamander will eat it. Many people simply leave the bottom of the tank bare, or use flat pieces of slate.

(Axolotls do need "hides," which helps them to manage stressful reactions by giving them a sense of security.)

Required Maintenance

Always remember that in keeping an aquatic life form as a pet, you are committing to maintaining the very atmosphere the creature breathes.

If you bring an axolotl into your life, you are looking at a long-term schedule of weekly water changes and water quality testing.

Consider how this will fit into your lifestyle, especially if you have to travel extensively for business. Who will care for your pet during those times? Or when you are away on vacation for a week or longer?

There is more specialized care involved in tending an axolotl than in changing a cat's litter box or walking a dog. What will your backup care plan entail?

Raising Your Own Food

Given the long-life of a well-cared for axolotl – as much as 15 years – you may find yourself in a position of raising your pet's food to keep costs down.

Options include cultivating earthworms, or setting up a second aquarium to raise aquatic blackworms or Daphnia (water fleas).

Neither is an expensive process, and will save a great deal of money over time on food for your pet, but these money-saving options do involve more work for you.

If you live at a great distance from large pet stores where typical axolotl foods can be purchased, you may have no choice but to raise live food for your pet.

(Food options for axolotls are discussed in full later in this chapter, with explanations of how these foods may be cultivated at home.)

Few Veterinarian Options

A lack of expert veterinarian assistance is a hurdle faced by many people who chose to keep exotic pets. This is particularly true, however, of an animal as unusual as an axolotl.

As discussed in the next chapter on axolotl health, many vets do not even know what these creatures are until an owner shows up in need of a consultation and treatment for their pet.

In many instances, you will be the one who is the expert on your pet's needs and potential illnesses and may be in a position of simply asking the vet for help in getting a test performed or administering a treatment that is outside your comfort range.

For the most part axolotls are healthy, hardy, long-lived pets, but they are subject to stress and highly dependent on good nutrition and good water quality. If you attend to those things properly, serious health issues should not arise.

If they do, however, you must be prepared for the fact that your chances of finding a veterinarian to assist you in caring for your pet are not good.

Most owners admit they self-diagnose health problems in their axolotls and turn to other owners in online discussion forums for advice and guidance.

Designing a Habitat

Axolotls are not demanding in terms of their accommodations. With a very basic "shopping list," you can create a suitable home for your pet at minimal expense.

Aquarium with Lid

One adult axolotl can be easily housed in a standard 10 gallon / 37.85 aquarium with dimensions of 20 x 10 x 10 inches (50 cm x 25 cm x 25 cm). Invest in a lid preferably mesh, to prevent instances of leaping.

These basic tanks are highly affordable, and can usually be acquired for less than $25 / £16.04.

A lid will add less than $10 / £6.41 to the cost.

Thermometer

You will want a thermometer to monitor water conditions, typically at a cost of approximately $5 / £3.20.

Shoot for optimal conditions in a range of 50-68 F (10-20 C). Anything below 50 F / 10 C will cause your axolotl's metabolism to slow down and become sluggish.

Temperatures above 77 F (25 C) will cause your pet to become stressed, with illness and disease inevitable.

Under these circumstances, if the temperature is not stabilized within two days, the axolotl will likely die.

Always try to keep the temperature in the tank steady, as fluctuations are just as stressful and harmful to your pet.

Filter and Water Flow

Technically, a filter is not essential to keep a pet axolotl, but there will be a lot of waste in the tank.

Using a filter cuts down on the necessary number of water changes, but you must choose carefully and get a unit that is exactly the right size for your tank.

An inexpensive unit like the Whisper PF10 Aquarium Filter (5-10 Gal) for $15 / £9.62 should do the job quite well. Axolotls don't like too much water flow, however. The movement stresses them out and makes them more susceptible to disease.

It's a good idea to find a way to disperse the outflow from the filter by either directing it against the side of the tank or having it flow over a rock.

You also have the option of using a spray bar, which will be sold as an attachment to an existing pump. These attachments often cost less than $1 / £0.64.

Some enthusiasts prefer to buy a more expensive filter that allows the rate of water exchange per hour to be raised and lowered.

Expect to pay approximately $30-$50 / £19.25-£32.09 for a pump with these control options.

Using Plants and a Hide Area

Live plants look nice in any tank, but axolotls will uproot them. You can try putting plants in small pots to anchor the bottom, and any floating plants are a good choice.

Many stem plants will also grow well floated. Some choices in the proper temperature range include

- Anacharis (Egeria densa), 50-83 F / 10-28 C, Cost: $2.69 / £1.72

- Hornwort or Coontail (Ceratophyllum demersum), 60-86 F / 15-30 C, Cost: $2.99 / £1.91

- Vallisneria (Vallisneria spp.), 60-86 F / 15-30 C, Cost: $6.99 / £4.47 for 10-12 plants

Plants will give the axolotl a sense of security, as will a "hide area." This can be something as simple as a broken piece of clay pipe or a flowerpot with a "door" knocked out of one side.

Nothing elaborate is required. Just think of it as creating a "man cave" for your pet.

Avoid anything that will leach chemicals into the water, including hard plastics that might contain toxic BPA.

Bottom Substrate

It's much better not to use normal aquarium gravel with axolotls. They can eat the material, develop intestinal blockages, and die. In order to achieve an aesthetic look, you can use aquarium sealant to glue some gravel in place.

Many people who keep axolotls opt for flat pieces of slate, fine sand, or a combination of both. It isn't necessary to put down any kind of substrate.

Typically fine aquarium sand sells for about $1 / £0.64 a pound / .45 kg.

Pieces of black slate are either sold by weight, or in lot numbers. For 12 pieces, expect to pay about $15 / £9.62.

You can allow your pet to live on the bare glass at the bottom of the tank, although some enthusiasts feel their axolotls can't get good traction on glass alone.

Cycling the Tank

Axolotls produce a lot of waste material, which quickly converts to toxic ammonia in the water.

To really create an environment conducive for good health, the tank should be aged two weeks before your pet is placed inside.

There are many ways to "cycle" your tank to establish the necessary nitrogen cycle. The following is only one simple method. If you are uncertain, consult the advice of a more experienced aquarist.

The Rudiments of Water Chemistry

Most aquarists will happily debate water quality to the point of being obsessive. Water is, after all, the atmosphere on which your pets depend.

It isn't necessary to have a degree in chemistry to maintain a healthy aquarium, but you will need to do some water testing.

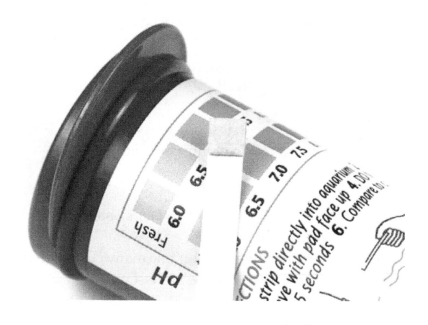

Axolotls are extremely sensitive to water quality. You must be prepared to test the water in your tank on a weekly basis to ensure your pet's continued good health.

With that in mind, there are some basic measurements you need to at least understand to some degree.

Acidity or Per Hydrogen (pH)

The "pH" sign for most people signals an assessment of acidity. When viewed as a scale, low numbers mean greater acidity and higher numbers indicate "basic" or alkaline water.

The actual measurement is the balance in the water between hydrogen (H+) and hydroxide (OH) ions. Axolotls are freshwater creatures, so they need a pH range of 6.5 to 7.5.

Carbonate Hardness (KH)

With this measurement, it's easy to confuse terms. KH refers to alkalinity, which is not the same thing as "alkaline."

Alkalinity is a description of the water's ability to neutralize and absorb acid, thereby acting as a "buffer." If the KH level in water is high, there won't be many changes in the pH level, and the water will be more stable.

Specific Gravity (sg)

In its most simple terms, specific gravity measures the salinity of water. It is taken with a hydrometer or a refractometer. Since axolotl are freshwater creatures, the specific gravity of their water should be around 1.0000.

Hard vs. Soft Water

Axolotls prefer slightly hard water. If you have limescale in your cookware or around your pipes, you have hard water.

If your axolotl is living in water that is too soft, its color will fade, especially the shade of the gills. This indicates your pet is suffering from temporary anemia. You will need to add salts to the water to increase the hardness.

Since these equations can be confusing, it's best to find out in advance if the water in your area is hard or soft and consult with an experienced aquarist about the best corrective measures to test.

The variance in water quality in this regard can be so extensive, there is no one set formula to "fix" the measurement. In general, however, soft water tends to be more acidic and hard water is more alkaline in terms of pH.

Understanding the Nitrogen Cycle

Creating the nitrogen cycle in an aquarium cultivates healthy bacteria in the water. Waste by-products create levels of ammonia that quickly become toxic to the tank's inhabitants.

In a cycled tank, nitrifying bacteria consume the ammonia and produce nitrite, which is in turn eaten by more bacteria and converted to nitrate.

A simple approach to establishing the nitrogen cycle involves putting household ammonia in the water until a level of 2-4 ppm is established. Test kits available at any pet store that sells aquarium supplies will help determine this number.

When the ammonia level is correct, put in a good amount of fish food and begin testing the water every 24 hours until the ammonia levels start to go down. That means nitrite is now present.

Bring the ammonia back up to 2-4 ppm and now test for both ammonia and nitrite. You want them both to drop. At the point at which you have 0 ppm of each, you should be able to get a nitrate reading. The water is then ready to support life forms.

Change about 70-90% of the water and get the nitrate level to less than 40 ppm before you introduce your axolotl to the tank.

Maintenance Considerations

The cleaner you keep the tank, the easier it will be to maintain good water quality.

Always use dechlorinated water and remove uneaten foods with a siphon or small aquarium vacuum.

A unit like the Aqueon Medium Siphon Vacuum Aquarium Gravel Cleaner retails for $7-$10 / £4.49-£6.41.

Every week, change out 10-20% of the water volume and get in the habit of testing the pH.

Feeding Requirements

Chapter 2 – Keeping Pet Axolotls

Axolotls have large, wide mouths, which they open quickly when they eat. This action creates a vacuum. The water rushes in drawing the food with it, and is sometimes so abrupt the axolotl will jump upwards in response.

Although they are carnivores, adult axolotls don't care if their food is alive or dead. When they are young, however, they will only eat live food.

At any stage of your pet's life, when you do use live foods, you must ensure that the food sources are not themselves carrying parasites or disease. Stay away from feeder fish for this reason.

Earthworms

Due to the longevity of axolotls in captivity, many enthusiasts simply raise earthworms to feed their pets. This is an economical solution, but even purchased from a commercial source, earthworms are inexpensive.
A typical online price range for 2000 "red wigglers" is $30 - $50 / £19.35 - £32.25.

A "kit" to set up your own worm farm, however, is just $50 - $60 / £32.25 - £38.70.

Worms can be fed on compost created from your kitchen garbage. This "do it yourself" solution will ensure that your axolotl always has a ready supply of food, and you always have plenty of bait on hand if you decide to go fishing!

Aquatic Blackworms

These worms are actually dark brown in coloration and are essentially the aquatic equivalent of the earthworm. Many people who keep pet axolotls consider blackworms a staple of their pet's diet.

Available in both freeze-dried and "flash" dried forms, expect to pay $40 / £25.80 for 3.52 ounces / 100 grams.

If you are feeding blackworms to young axolotls, the creatures must be live or the babies won't eat them. Young axolotls are highly carnivorous, to the point that they'll even take a bite out of one another!

One pound / 0.45 kg of live blackworms costs approximately $40 / £25.80.

Raising your own blackworms is somewhat more complicated than cultivating earthworms, but is far from impossible or even impractical if you are willing to put in a little extra work.

You would need a separate 5-10 gallon / 18.92 – 37.85 liter aquarium filled with 5 inches / 12.7 cm of water over approximately 2 inches / 5.08 cm of gravel substrate.

The tank should be outfitted with an air pump and kept at room temperature. Stock the tank with live blackworms you've purchased as breeding stock, and feed them fresh produce and fish food every other day.

Feed only as much as the population will consume during the interval between scheduled feedings. You will have to monitor your tank to determine the correct amount.

Change out half of the water on a weekly basis. Use only dechlorinated water. When algae sprouts in the tank, leave it there. The worms will eat it.

Restock the tank as needed with purchased replacement worms.

Bloodworms

Bloodworms are a nutritious staple and easily obtained in freeze-dried form since they are often used to feed tropical fish.

Expect to pay $5 / £3.22 for .28 oz / 8 grams.

Daphnia

Daphnia (water fleas) can be used as a staple food, and brine shrimp are highly nutritious and easy to acquire. You can also try sinking salmon pellets, but not all axolotl will eat them.

Although prices will vary widely by pet store and food type, as an example, a bag of live Daphnia typically costs $10 / £6.41.

Daphnia, however, offer the unique advantage of being able to actually live in the aquarium with your axolotl without fouling the water until they are consumed.

To raise Daphnia at home, obtain live Daphnia and introduce them to a standard 5 gallon / 18.92 liter aquarium placed under a light source and outfitted with a slow bubbling air stone, not a filter.

Aquarium air stones are inexpensive, with a pack of five selling for $5 - $6 / £3.22 - £3.87.

Mix one package of dry yeast with one cup of soy flour. Stir one-eighth to one-quarter of a teaspoon of the mixture in a cup of warm water and pour it into the aquarium to serve as food for the Daphnia.

Do not feed the Daphnia again until the water becomes clear, which is an indication that all of the feed mixture has been consumed.
Combine water changes with harvesting. Scoop out Daphnia-filled water and strain the creatures out of the old water, which you will then discard.

Put the Daphnia in the tank with your axolotl, and introduce clean, dechlorinated water into your daphnia tank.

Clean the bottom of the Daphnia tank with an aquarium vacuum as needed, generally every other week.

Pellet Fish Foods

For convenience sake, pellet fish foods are a solid nutritional source as long as the item chosen has a good balance of protein and vitamins.

Try for a mix of 45% protein, with fat content of no more than 20%.

For young axolotls, find a pellet that is roughly 0.3 cm / 3 mm. Adults should not be fed pellets larger than 0.5 cm / 5 mm.

Other Food Choices

Brine shrimp can be used as a staple food, but since they are difficult to grow at home, they can become expensive.

When purchased frozen, brine shrimp have a tendency to foul the water, which creates more of a maintenance nightmare for you.

Most enthusiasts offer brine shrimp as an occasional special meal in order to cut down on the resulting mess. The same is true of commercial newt and turtle food.

Neither of these prepared foods has enough of the correct nutritional content to be fed exclusively to an axolotl, but some axolotls seem to enjoy these floating foods.

Remember, however, that all axolotls are individuals and they will tell you what they do and don't like. If you try a floating food and your pet doesn't touch it, he's not interested. Don't waste your money again.

Foods to Avoid

Any food that is high in fat content is inappropriate for an axolotl and can be the cause of liver disease.

Many people new to keeping these pets choose whiteworms because their axolotl seems to like them so much. This is a mistake.

As an occasional treat, whiteworms are fine for adults, but they have far too much fat content to be a staple item.

They can, however, be fed to growing juveniles for a limited period of time. The same is true of any form of grub.

It's also best to avoid feeder fish unless you are absolutely certain they are not carrying parasites – a determination that is almost impossible to make.

Your axolotl will have a fine time "hunting" feeder fish, but do this very sparingly as the risk is too great in most cases.

Axolotls enjoy mealworms, which are very easy to obtain due to their popularity as reptile food. One or two is fine, but the axolotl cannot digest the mealworm's exoskeleton, which will be expelled in the water.

If you feed your pet mealworms, you have to be on the lookout for the exoskeleton and get it out of the tank before it fouls the water. This extra maintenance alone is a good reason to keep the use of mealworms to the bare minimum.

Hand Feeding Your Axolotl

There really is no trick to "teaching" an axolotl to eat out of your hand. Remember, that cute little guy sitting at the bottom of your tank is a predator by nature. If you hold food in front of his mouth and he's hungry, he will go for it.

Don't worry about being bitten. Axolotls only have stubby little bumps for "teeth." They can grip, but they can't bite and they certainly can't break human skin. At most, you'll be startled and feel a little pressure.

If your pet seems reluctant to take what you're holding out, wiggling it a little as if the food were bait. The motion will activate the axolotl's hunting instinct. If you want your pet to consistently take food from your hand, offer it at the same time every day.

It's perfectly easy to just drop food in the aquarium and let the axolotl eat on its own, but then it will become accustomed to doing so and be less likely to eat from your hand.

Because axolotls are both intelligent and observant, they will quickly become accustomed to scheduled feedings by hand and even look forward to it.

Don't be surprised if your pet stands up on its hind legs as you approach the tank in anticipation of the hand-fed meal – or even "bangs" on the glass with its paw to tell you to hurry up!

Remember to always wash and thoroughly rinse your hands before interacting with your axolotl in this fashion. The primary rule of good care for these aquatic pets is to maintain optimum water quality at all times.

Any residue on your hands can change the chemical composition of the water and prove potentially toxic to the axolotl.

Obviously, you will also want to wash your hands after they've been in the tank as well, since properly cycled aquarium water does contain bacteria.

Tank Mates

Trying to house axolotl with any creature but their own kind is not a good idea. Anything that is smaller and moves is fair game in the axolotl's carnivore mind.

By the same token, don't house axolotls 3 inches (8 cm) and smaller together in a confined space, or they will turn carnivorous. Some "nipping" behavior will continue until the creatures grow beyond 6 inches (15-16 cm).

Cannibalistic tendencies are less prevalent in axolotls that have been bred for specific color variations, although no one knows why. In adults, the issue disappears, however.

Pros and Cons of Owning an Axolotl

As with most pets, the pros and cons of owning an axolotl are relative to the owner. Some people wouldn't own a dog because they don't want to walk their pet. Others get a dog for that very reason.

For some people even the idea of keeping a pet salamander has an "ick" factor, but axolotls have a highly unique charm. They are not menacing in appearance and one of the first thing people new to the species notice is their slight, almost quixotic "smile."

The main "negative" issue with axolotls is tank maintenance. Even if you are feeding something as simple as earthworms, there will be debris in the tank that must be cleaned up so the water doesn't foul.

Weekly water changes are necessary to prevent a buildup of toxic ammonia, and most experts recommend testing the water regularly.

A product like Tetra EasyStrips 6-in-1 Test Strips can be purchased in lots of 100 for as little as $20 / £12.83, but this will be an ongoing expense for the life of the axolotl.

On the pro side, however, axolotls are interesting exotic pets that live well in a contained environment. Although not the sort of creatures that can be handled due to their fragile skin and totally aquatic existence, they are fascinating and they do have distinct personalities.

They can and do learn to recognize their owners, and in their own way, they are interactive. Additionally, they have a long lifespan of up to 15 years and are, on a whole, quite hardy and healthy when they receive the proper care.

Estimated Cost of Owning an Axolotl

The cost of the axolotl itself will vary widely. Some pet stores will sell specimens for as little as $10 / £6.41, while breeders may ask as much as $100 / £64.18.

From there, the basic set-up supplies include the following:

10 gallon / 37.85 liter aquarium with lid
Cost: under $35 / £22.46

Thermometer
Cost: $5 / £3.20

Basic Filter
$15 / £9.62 (simple model with no controls)
spray bar attachment for a filter $1 / £0.64

Estimated Cost of Owning an Axolotl

Advanced Filter
$30-$50 / £19.25-£32.09
(with controls for regulate rate of water exchange per hour)

live plants
$5-$10 / £3.20-£6.41
some structure to serve as a "hide" area
less than $10 / £6.41

Substrate
fine aquarium sand at $1 / £0.64 a pound / .45kg or black
slate at $15 / £9.62 for approximately 12 pieces

aquarium siphon "vacuum"
$7-$10 / £4.49-£6.41

food, varies by type

aquarium test strips
lot of 100 - $20 / £12.83

Depending on prices and availability in your area, you
should be able to acquire one axolotl and outfit its habitat
for $150-$175 / £96.27-£112.32.

Summary: Feeding Guide

In captivity, axolotl health depends mainly on two factors: good nutrition and water quality. By nature, these animals are extremely hardy.

If you feed your pet a varied diet taken from the acceptable sources listed below, and maintain a clean, chemically sound environment for the axolotl, you can expect to have your pet with you for many years.

Good Food Sources

Earthworms
Aquatic blackworms
Bloodworms
Daphnia (water fleas)
Pellet fish food
Brine shrimp

Questionable Food Sources

Whiteworms
Feeder fish
Mealworms

Foods You Can Raise at Home

Earthworms
Aquatic blackworms
Daphnia (water fleas)

Summary: Feeding Guide

Avoid foods high in fat content, and anything that seriously fouls the water.

Test ammonia levels weekly and remove all uneaten food within a couple of hours of feeding your pet.

Chapter 3 – Axolotl Health and Breeding

For the most part, axolotls are healthy pets with a remarkably long lifespan of as much as 15 years. Part of their attractiveness as a companion animal is their low maintenance profile.

To keep an axolotl in optimum health, pay attention to its tank conditions both by testing the water on a weekly basis and by simply observing your pet.

Water Quality is Crucial

The most important thing you can do to ensure the health of your Axolotl is to maintain the water quality in its tank. Start with dechlorinated water

---

Chlorine Poisoning

Signs of chlorine poisoning in a pet axolotl are quite clear. The creature will tremble and its color will shift, generally become paler. Respiration will increase markedly, and the axolotl will try to get out of the tank – help him do so!

If you suspect chlorine in the water, remove the axolotl to a chlorine-free tank immediately. Change out all the water in the original tank, making sure you've used dechlorinated water.

This will mean that your pet will have to live in a tank without an established nitrogen cycle until you get the water in the first tank back in good shape.

Test the water in the secondary tank daily and do not let toxic levels of ammonia build up.

Maintaining Water Quality

In maintaining the quality of your pet's watery home, you will want to pay particular attention to the following factors.

- Maintain good water chemistry.

It is crucial to prevent the build-up of ammonia in the tank, and to keep the pH level stable. Like many creatures that live in aquariums, axolotls do not tolerate severe fluctuations in water quality.

- Regulate tank temperature for degree and stability.

Although there will be times when you want to change the temperature in your pet's home, lowering it to facilitate wound healing or to slow down the development of young axolotls, any such changes must be done gradually.

Overheating will kill these sensitive creatures very quickly. The best temperature range is 50-68 F (10-20 C). Never allow the tank to heat above 77 F (25 C).

- Limit the amount of water movement.

Axolotls do not like water movement at all and can be severely stressed if subjected to a current.

Always direct the outflow from the filter against a surface to disperse its energy and keep the water as still as possible.

(Consult the previous chapter for more detail on correct tank parameters and conditions.)

Consequences of Stress

If your axolotl is suffering from heat or water stress, it will begin to refuse food and may develop pale patches on the skin coated in a mucus-like material. Often the axolotl's coloration will begin to fade, especially on the gills.

Because the axolotl is highly aware of the environment outside its tank, and may interpret movement or changes in light as the presence of a predator, you must provide your pet with a place to hide. This alone will significantly decrease the stress to which it can be subject.

Sometimes axolotl's develop gas, which will cause them to float in the tank. Always immediately decrease the water level so the creature can touch the bottom of the tank while remaining submerged. If you allow the axolotl to continue floating, it will only suffer from increased stress levels.

Potential Treatments

When an axolotl does become ill and its condition is not improved by correcting issues of temperature and water chemistry, there is often little that can be done for your pet.

Some conditions you might encounter include:

- Fluid retention or edema. This can be caused by damage to the heart or kidneys, nutritional deficiencies, or simple old age.

- Tumor growth. There is, unfortunately, a great deal of inbreeding among captive axolotls, which causes genetic abnormalities. In these cases, nature will simply take its course.

- Physical injuries. As long as the water is kept very clean and no infection sets in, axolotls heal extremely well — to the point of being able to regenerate whole limbs.

Interestingly, their wound healing is faster at lower temperatures, so you may want to bring the water slowly down to a range of 41-59 F / 5-15 C.

(Never make rapid changes in water temperature as this is a severe stressor for axolotls.)

- Bacterial infections. The most common of this type of illness is "red leg" bacteria, aptly names since it manifests with red patches on the legs and body.

Chapter 3 – Axolotl Health and Breeding

Change the water in the tank and treat the salamander in a salt bath once or twice a day. Use 2-3 teaspoons of common salt per two pints of water.

Do not use a higher concentration of salt, or you run the risk of damaging the creature's sensitive gills.

For most fungal and bacterial infections, salt baths will do the trick. In severe cases, a few drops of Mercurochrome in the water will also help.

Use only enough to tint the water slightly orange. This treatment is also effective if you suspect your axolotl has parasites.

Typically if parasites are an issue, the axolotl will excrete a mucous like substance from the skin or will appear to behave in an agitated manner

Certainly you can try any of the recommended aquarium treatments for fungal, bacterial, and parasitical infections.

Do NOT, however, use the following products:

- Sterazin
- Cuprazin
- Protozin
- Clout
- Rid Rot
- Any product listing "malachite green" as an ingredient.

Treatment products that are considered safe for use with axolotls include:

- Myxazin
- The Complete Remedy
- Mercurochrome
- Nitrofura-G
- Maracyn
- Tetra Sulfa Bath
- Methylene Blue
- Furan-2
- Melafix
- Pancur
- Flagyl

Of these, Furan-2 is highly recommended for a broad range of bacterial infections, Melafix is especially good for external sores, and Panacur will work against internal parasites.

Signs of Disease

The best preventive health measure you can take for your axolotl is your own active involvement in its life. No one will know what is "normal" for your pet but you.

If you think something is wrong, it probably is. Be especially vigilant for the following signs of disease:

- Loss of appetite. An axolotl can survive for as long as three weeks without eating, but if it begins to obviously lose body mass, something is not right.

- Lethargic movements. Axolotls are capable of rather amazing bursts of speed. They are also capable of sitting very still, but if they do this for hours and days on end, the behavior is not normal.

- Changes to the gills. Any change in the color or quality of the gills, including visible decay of the fine threads is a clear indicator of illness. This includes gill direction. If the gills are turned forward, the creature is experiencing stress.

- Floating. If an axolotl is incapable of remaining at the bottom of the tank, it likely has gas from a gastrointestinal issue.

- Loss of color. If fed improperly, axolotls can develop anemia, which manifests with loss of body color.

- Open sores or mucous. Some bacterial and fungal infections will cause open wounds or sores and the secretion of a mucous-like substance.

- Gasping for breath. Rapid respiration that resembles panting is a sign of both stress and illness.

Most health problems are seen in juvenile axolotls. Once the creature attains full maturity at age 18 months to two years, it should be quite stable if its environment is well maintained.

Additional Health Conditions

Axolotls are, by nature, incredibly healthy and capable of almost super "human" feats of regeneration and healing. If injured, their limbs will regrow perfect and indistinguishable copies. No scar tissue will be present.

Like any animal kept in captivity, however, they can be the victims of inappropriate conditions and diet that even their robust constitutions cannot overcome.

Metabolic Bone Disease

Metabolic Bone Disease is the umbrella term for a series of health-related problems in pet axolotls, all tied to nutritional deficiencies or imbalances.

Symptoms of MBD may not surface until the problem is advanced, and can include:

- curvature of the spine
- broken bones
- fluid retention and bloating
- jaw deformities that prevent the mouth from closing
- lethargic behavior
- trembling and / or spasms
- intestinal prolapse

Since all of these symptoms can be attributed to other causes, MBD in axolotls is often mistaken for another condition and left untreated.

An X-ray will likely be required for an accurate diagnosis. While a small animal veterinarian may not be familiar with axolotls or amphibians in general, most will be willing to take an X-ray if you help them to understand what you're trying to discover.

Be prepared, however, that the vet may need to consult with a colleague, often someone teaching at a college of veterinary medicine, to be able to interpret the X-ray findings.

Most veterinarians are willing to at least attempt to estimate charges in advance for tests of this sort. Call and describe the situation and ask for such an estimate before going into the clinic. In the vast majority of cases, whether you receive treatment or not, you will be charged for any in-office visits.

If MBD is suspected, most axolotl owners try to correct the problem, or at least improve it, by changing their pet's diet.

The nutritional deficiencies or imbalances that underlie a case of MBD include:

- lack of calcium
- Vitamin D deficiency
- phosphor imbalance
- Vitamin A deficiency

The best safeguard against and cure for metabolic bone disease is feeding your axolotl a proper diet that mimics, in so much as it is possible, what the creature would eat in its wild state.

A diet that includes fresh live food and vitamin and mineral fortified commercial food is recommended, with no high fat content.

If you are using freeze-dried or flash frozen foods in quantity, consider incorporating more live content in the axolotl's diet.

The freezing process, though convenient for shipping and storage, does reduce the nutritional quality of the foods in question.

Toxins or Poisons in the Water

The reason this text continues to emphasize water quality is that no single factor will more directly affect the health of your axolotl.

Pay particular attention to the color and size of the creature's feathery gills. If they begin to turn pale, or to shrink, something is wrong with the water.

The most likely culprits are carbon dioxide poisoning from a lack of oxygen in the water and a build-up of toxic ammonia.

Nitrate poisoning is also a possibility. Any time your axolotl shows a diminished appetite, changed body color, and changed gill size or behavior, look to water quality first.

The best preventive and corrective measures are using a good quality air filter and testing the chemical composition of the water on a weekly basis.

Always remember to divert the outflow from the filter to minimize movement of the water in the tank. Aeration is necessary for tank health, but overly agitating the water is very bad for your pet.

Stress from water movement is difficult for an axolotl to tolerate. A key indicator of ill health from water movement is gill position.

Usually if the gills appear to be swept forward, there's too much current in the tank and your pet is feeling the negative effect of the water's motion.

An Axolotl Vet?

A veterinarian participating in the leading axolotl authoritative website, Caudata.org, neatly summarized the problem of professional healthcare for many exotic pets.

"I am a small animal vet and I have seen an increasing number of clients bringing in exotics (reptiles / amphibians / arachnids / insects), and I must admit, I wasn't prepared. Many of my vet colleagues too are not familiar with exotics medicine, and we all tend to refer the client to a specialist."

In the discussion that followed, most axolotl owners admitted they self-diagnose their pets, or turn to enthusiast communities online to hash out the problem and arrive at a possible solution.

Some members said they had consulted vets, only to be referred to a specialist while still incurring a consultation fee for a visit that did nothing to help their pet. Several said their vets didn't even know what an axolotl was when asked for their medical advice.

That being said, many conscientious vets do try their best. Another veterinarian joined in the discussion, describing attempts to correctly diagnose and treat an axolotl with a lesion on its flank.

"I felt very crippled by this stage," he said, after listing off the process of obtaining a specimen for testing via fine needle biopsy. "I'm not exactly familiar with the specific pathogens of amphibians and had to discuss the case with my colleagues and research the net and textbooks."

At the end of his post, this second vet said that very case drove him to join the discussion forum, where he learned invaluable information from the members themselves.

Essentially, axolotl owners are likely going to be on their own when it comes to treating their pets. In a best-case scenario, you may be able to approach a vet to help you perform a procedure, like giving an injection, or to complete a test like a biopsy as described above.

This is a daunting aspect of keeping an exotic pet, and one for which you must be prepared. On a whole, axolotls are very healthy, but if a problem does arise, you may well be the only "doctor" called in to attend the case.

Axolotl Breeding

Most axolotls can breed after 18 months of age. Although mating tends to occur early in the year, it can happen at any time.

Females who are ready to mate will appear more rounded at the end of their body. It's often extremely difficult to tell the genders apart, so if you are housing two axolotls, be prepared for just about anything!

Females lay as many as a thousand eggs at a time, and need at least 2-3 months in a tank alone to recover from the strain of the experience. If you are certain of the gender of your pets, there are ways you can stimulate breeding.

Encouraging Reproduction

Keep your axolotls in a room that receives enough light for the creatures to have a perception of the seasonal changes. Their mating instinct responds to both light and slight temperature fluctuations.

If you want your axolotls to breed, provide plenty of plants on which the females can affix their eggs. Use flat slate or other stone in the bottom of the tank as a substrate to assist the males in depositing their spermatophores.

These cone-shaped structures are like jelly in consistency and contain a packet of sperm. They will not stick to either glass or plastic.

The male axolotl initiates the spawning by swimming around the tank with his tail raised. He will make writhing motions and may approach the female to nudge her vent.

He will have deposited anywhere from 5 to 25 spermatophores around the tank, and will attempt to lead the female over them until she picks one up in her cloaca.

Sometime in the next few hours or days, she will begin to deposit her eggs on every available surface. When she is clearly finished, remove the eggs from the tank.

Hatching Axolotl Eggs

Although axolotl larvae are very tough and can survive almost anything, don't try to raise the large numbers your female has deposited.

Cull the eggs down to 100 or so, sharing the eggs with other enthusiasts. (Eggs are often traded or sold on salamander forums online.)

Transfer the eggs to a secondary tank you have prepared expressly for hatching. If possible, simply remove the entire plant or structure on which the eggs are affixed. If you have to severe the attachment, you can do so with nothing more than the edge of your fingernail.

Place the eggs in a small aquarium measuring around 18" x 8" x 10" / 45 x 20 x 25 cm. Make sure the water is well aerated, but follow the usual strictures against water movement. Always disperse the outflow from the filter.

If the eggs are kept in 64 F / 18 C water, they will hatch in 20 days. This is a good thing if you suddenly have eggs to tend unexpectedly as you will need time to acquire the necessary foods. Newly hatched axolotls must be fed live food. They won't eat anything that doesn't move.

When they first hatch, the remains of the egg yolk will still be present in their stomachs, but the young will need to be fed within 24-72 hours.

Good choices for food are newly hatched brine shrimp or small Daphnia (water fleas). Plan on feeding twice a day. The developmental stage for axolotl involves five stages:

Stage 1 - The egg, roughly 2 mm in size, containing an embryo surrounded by layers of jelly.

Stage 2 - The embryo just prior to hatching, at a size of 11 mm.

Stage 3 - Young larva before any limbs are present.

Stage 4 - Larva aged two weeks, with the front legs beginning to be visible.

Stage 5 - A fully formed, miniature axolotl.

When the young reach a length of 2 cm, they become cannibalistic and will need to be divided by size. Larger specimens will prey on smaller ones.

Do not be surprised if you have to thin out deformed or sick specimens from the growing larvae. Genetic abnormalities are common in this species due to the high level of inbreeding in captivity.

If you are caught unawares and suddenly have a large number of babies on the way, immediately start finding prospective homes — or buy a lot of aquariums!

Summary: Axolotl Health

Finding a veterinarian to treat an axolotl is extremely difficult. In most cases, owners self-diagnose and turn to other enthusiasts online for advice and assistance.

Signs of Illness

Loss of appetite
Lethargy
Changes to the gills
Floating
Loss of color
Open sores and mucous
Labored or rapid respiration
Coming to the surface to breathe

Conditions Related to Water Quality

Chlorine poisoning
Carbon dioxide poisoning
Nitrate poisoning
Stress related to water movement
Heat stress

Other Common Health Conditions

Fluid retention / edema
Metabolic bone disease
Bacterial infections
Fungal growths

Summary: Axolotl Health

Tumors
Physical injuries

Any time you suspect that your axolotl is ill, always address issues of water quality first. In most cases, improving the chemical composition of the water will solve the attendant health problem.

Chapter 4 - Axolotls and Medical Research

Chapter 4 - Axolotls and Medical Research

While it may seem odd to talk about medical research in a book devoted to the keeping of axolotls as pets, these creatures are fulfilling a unique role on the cutting edge of medical investigations in cell regeneration.

There are large colonies of axolotls housed solely for research purposes, and it is true that the animals kept in laboratories are subject to amputations and transplants. The debate over the moral implications of the use of laboratory animals is intense and highly personal for animal rights advocates.

It is not the purpose of this narrative to come down on either side of that argument, only to discuss why axolotls are being used in medical research and what goals those programs have in mind in terms of their potential benefit to mankind.

Much of the work being done with axolotls focuses on outcomes similar to those set for research efforts with human stem cells, another highly controversial avenue of investigation, and one even more fraught with moral and religious potholes.

Oddly enough, were the axolotl not prized by researchers, the species might already have passed into extinction. Axolotls do possess amazing healing abilities, and they are the focus of groundbreaking medical efforts. It is up to you, the reader, to judge for yourself the "rightness" or "wrongness" of these investigations.

The Potential for Cell Regeneration

Compared to the state of medical treatment a hundred, fifty, or even 25 years ago, miracles are being worked by doctors and nurses on a daily basis.

However, the limitations of that same science are maddening in their elusiveness. True cell regeneration is one of those limitations, so sought after that some medical researchers refer to it as the "Holy Grail."

Axolotls may be the unlikely knights that find that elusive healing chalice. These remarkable creatures don't just have the ability to regenerate lost limbs. They can grow back missing portions of their brain and spinal cord. Organs taken from one axolotl and transplanted into another function perfectly with no sign of rejection.

This is not a one shot deal, or even a hat trick. An axolotl can perform this process literally hundreds of times with no evidence of scar tissue and no way to distinguish the new limb from the one it is replacing.

Is Human Cell Regeneration Possible?

Humans are descended from amphibians. Very young children can regenerate lost finger tips, but as we age, this ability disappears. Researchers hope that by studying axolotls they can learn how to reactivate this ability. The implications are staggering.

New treatments could ease the now excruciating recovery and life-altering scarring from severe burns. Regenerated nerves might enable paraplegics and quadriplegics to regain their mobility. Amputees could possibly be able to regrow their own lost limbs.

The harmful scarring from heart and liver surgery could be a thing of the past, and transplant recipients might no longer fear the tragedy of organ rejection. Axolotls may even hold the key to curing cancer. They are a thousand times more resistant to cancer than any species of mammal.

Chapter 4 - Axolotls and Medical Research

Not only do axolotls intrigue researchers working with disease cures and wound healing, they also raise the potential for anti-aging treatments, an ever-attractive proposition for we vain human beings.

How Do Axolotls Regenerate Tissue?

Until recently scientists thought that when an axolotl suffered a wound, the cells at the site differentiated to attain the kind of pluripotentiality seen in human stem cells. When an axolotl sustains a wound, coagulation is instantaneous. It is almost as if the pace of the healing is visible to the human eye.

A protective covering forms over the wound and creates the living foundation for the subsequent limb regeneration. This covering, called a"blastema," was thought to be site of the evolution of pluripotent cells. This is not the case, however.

In 2009, a research team at the Max Planck Institute of Molecular Cell Biology and Genetics in Dresden published its findings in the medical journal "Nature" refuting this long held theory.

Using fluorescent proteins to make individual cells visible, the researchers found that no pluripotent cells formed in an axolotl's blastema. Regenerated cells in the newly formed limb developed from like progenitor cells in the wound. Muscle cells made new muscles, bone cells made new bones, and so forth.

Another research team at the Australian Regenerative Medicine Institute at Monash University in Melbourne discovered that if special cells called macrophages are removed in the early stages of axolotl healing, regeneration halts and scar tissue begins to form.

Although the pieces of the puzzle remain incomplete, every new understanding about the behavior of cell regeneration in axolotls provides information that is being applied to enhanced wound treatment in humans.

International Axolotl Research

There are numerous centers for axolotl research around the world. In September 2010, the Axolotl Center was founded at the Hanover Medical School in Germany. There, amphibian expert Christina Allmeling developed an international breeding program to save the endangered axolotl.

Allmeling is also dedicated to the principle that no animal should be killed for the sake of research. Through her efforts, the axolotls with which the Center works are given a stress-free retirement when their participation in the project is judged to be over.

Since younger axolotls heal more quickly, elderly specimens are removed from the program and cared for in their old age.

Research is also being conducted with axolotls at the Center for Regenerative Therapies at the Dresden University of Technology, the University of California-Irvine's Limb Regeneration program in the Department of Developmental and Cell Biology, and at the University of Kentucky among many others.

Surveying Axolotls in the Wild

It is truly ironic that medical research has proved to be the saving grace for the endangered axolotl species. Their status in the wild is quite dire, especially since invasive tilapias have been introduced into the few water systems where wild axolotls can still be found.

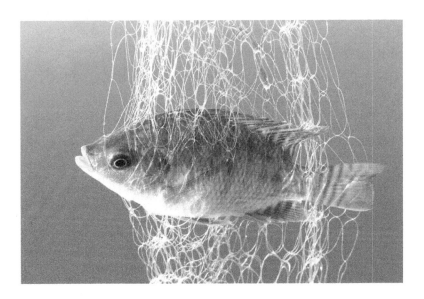

Twenty years ago the Mexican government introduced Tilapia and carp into the axolotl's only native habitat — the network of polluted canals that form the sad modern-day remnants of Lake Xochimilco in and around Mexico City.

In a metropolis where unemployment is chronically high, the thought was to supply local fishermen with a ready source of free food. The tilapia, however, reproduce much faster than they are harvested and feed voraciously on the plants axolotls need to lay their eggs. The resulting population decline for the axolotl is reaching critical mass.

The National Autonomous University of Mexico conducted an axolotl survey in 2012. The researchers found a population density of no more than 100 axolotls per square kilometer.

Chapter 4 - Axolotls and Medical Research

In 2004, the number was 10 times higher; another six times higher in the 1980s. Mexico City, the world's largest metropolitan area, is proving to be the doom of the wild axolotl.

Conservationists are working not just to save the axolotl, but to rehabilitate Lake Xochimilco as well.

Farmers are being encouraged to use more traditional methods of agriculture in an effort to keep pesticides and fertilizers out of the water, and entrances to some canals have been blocked to create tilapia-free zones for the axolotls.

Tracking devices on axolotls captured and released for study purposes show that the creatures are very active in their wild state, and they are discovering the new canal sanctuaries, a hopeful sign for those working on their behalf.

Other efforts are focused on creating an artificial lake an hour outside Mexico City at Tecamac in hopes of establishing a new home for transplanted axolotls. A group of axolotls bred in the lab are under observation as potential "colonists" in the new lake.

If they can effectively hunt water bugs and natural prey, these axolotls might be the very pioneers that settle a new wild habitat for a species the Aztecs believed were a god transformed — a deity with special powers to transform itself and elude sacrifice.

Fostering Retired Axolotls

While many enthusiasts express an interest in serving as caregivers for axolotls retired from medical research, labs and medical supply companies are quite adamant that they are not part of the pet trade in this species.

It is not uncommon for researchers themselves to grow fond of and care for retired axolotls that once participated in their laboratory work.

That being said, there is no harm in contacting any research facility and offering your services to care for a retired axolotl.

Chapter 4 - Axolotls and Medical Research

There is no guarantee of success; in fact, you will likely be told no, but your chances will be enhanced if you can prove your commitment to the species and illustrate a working knowledge of proper axolotl care.

If you are indeed a passionate advocate for these animals, ask if there is anything you can do to prove your suitability as a foster caregiver, or offer to contribute monetarily to the upkeep of retired research specimens.

Afterword

In many ways the axolotl is a surprising creature. With its feathered gills rising on either side of an amazingly expressive face, this "Mexican Walking Fish" is like no aquarium creature you've ever seen.

Arguably an evolutionary step backward as it is an amphibian that cannot leave the water, the axolotl remains in a larval stage throughout its life.

This neotenous existence may well have been a survival adaptation, allowing the creatures to remain safely out of the reach of predators.

This characteristic, paired with the axolotls amazing ability to re-grow limbs — and even its brain and spinal cord — have made the animals highly prized in medical research.

This may be one of the few cases where medical use has saved a species. Left in the wild, the axolotl might well have been rendered extinct by the destruction of its native habitat in the once-present freshwater lakes around Mexico City.

Little remains of those lakes now but polluted canals, and consequently, wild axolotls are on the CITES endangered species list. The little creatures, closely related to the Tiger Salamander, are widely bred in captivity both for research and the pet trade.

Afterword

Although axolotls are carnivores that cannot be housed with other species, they do well in pairs and have surprisingly few maintenance requirements. The essentials are good water quality, lack of stress (including that created by excessive water movement), and appropriate and constant temperature.

If cared for properly, a pet axolotl can live as long as 15 years. In that time, to the surprise of many new owners, your little pet will learn to recognize you and will interact with you.

Highly observant of their surroundings, axolotls will stand up on their hind legs and ask for attention, and use their paws against the glass to offer greetings, or, to seemingly ask questions.

In fact, their whimsical, half smiling faces are so expressive it does seem as if they will offer an opinion about something at any moment. Offer them food by hand, and they'll take it willingly — and generally ask for more.

If you are looking for an unusual pet to keep in an aquarium environment that is both exotic and reasonably low maintenance, an axolotl could well be the creature for you. They're certainly a fine conversation piece, just be prepared to answer one question a lot. "What IS that thing?"

Appendix 1 - Overview of Tiger Salamanders

Note: Since enthusiasts new to keeping pet amphibians often become confused about axolotls and tiger salamanders, we are providing an overview of tiger salamander care just in case you discover your axolotl isn't an axolotl at all!

The Tiger Salamander, in its larval stage closely resembles the axolotl, and the two animals are often mistaken for one another. Although related, and likely descended from a common source, the two salamanders are quite different.

(Interestingly enough, axolotls and tiger salamanders can successfully interbreed, although the practice is not encouraged.)

Appendix 1 - Overview of Tiger Salamanders

Tiger Salamanders (Ambystoma tigrinum) are, like the axolotl, long-lived amphibians with a tendency to exhibit neoteny, never metamorphosing into their adult form. In axolotls, however, neoteny is the norm; in tiger salamanders it's an aberration.

Many of the enthusiasts who claim to have an axolotl that has metamorphosed are actually keeping a tiger salamander without realizing it. If this has happened to you, the two species require a different standard of care depending on their stage of life, a fact for which you will have to be prepared.

Physical Characteristics

Tiger salamanders reach an adult length of 8-13 inches / 20.32-33.02 cm. They can have a lifespan as long as 25 years when cared for properly.

There are several subspecies indigenous to North America. All display some variation on a black body marked with yellow bars, spots, or paint-like patches. The patterns and color intensity are different, but all are quite striking.

The principle subspecies kept as pets are:

- Eastern Tiger Salamander: Found from New York to the eastern coast of Florida and westward to Kansas, Nebraska, and parts of East Texas, these creatures are black with yellow and olive spots arranged in roughly symmetrical band patterns. The subspecies is not present in the Appalachian highlands.

- Barred Tiger Salamander: This variety lives from Nebraska through southern Texas and west to central Colorado and New Mexico. They are marked with vertical bars in shades of yellow and tan against a dark brown to black background.

- Arizona Tiger Salamander: Ranging from southern Alberta, Canada to Colorado and Nebraska, this subspecies has a pattern of thin, dark markings that look like a gray or olive net on a darker background. Isolated populations are also present in western Washington and eastern Idaho.

These creatures are found in lakes and rivers throughout North America, and are endangered in the wild. Like the axolotl, however, they are widely bred in captivity. In most states where the species is present, it is illegal to capture a specimen in the wild.

If you are interested in keeping a tiger salamander as a pet, make sure you are obtaining a captive-bred animal from a legitimate breeder.

Personality and Behavior

Tiger salamanders are surprisingly interactive and engaging pets. They have very acute senses, including excellent vision. Although they are nocturnal and will be shy during the day, they do come to recognize their human keepers.

Appendix 1 - Overview of Tiger Salamanders

Due to the sensitivity of the tiger salamander's skin, do not try to hold your pet.

As your tiger salamander is growing, it will shed its skin via molting every few weeks. Do not be concerned as this is perfectly normal. The salamander will eat the cast off skin.

Required Habitat for Larval Stage

In their larval stage, tiger salamanders are, like axolotls, aquatic. They will fare well in a 10 gallon / 37.85 liter aquarium with a lid.

Fill the tank with approximately 6 inches / 15.24 cm of water. Provide rocks so the creatures have a place to hide, and use a slow bubbling air stone rather than a filter.

While not as sensitive to water motion as axolotls, tiger salamanders have sensitive skin that is easily irritated. Keep the temperature at 65 F - 70 F / 18 C - 21 C.

After several months, the larval tiger salamander will lose its gills. At this time, you need to reduce the water level in the tank slowly and provide a "land" area for the creature to transition to live in a terrestrial tank (terrarium).

Required Habitat for Adults

A tank of the same size will work well for an adult salamander. Continue to use a lid.

Adults like to burrow, so use a substrate in the bottom of their terrarium like potting soil, bark chips, sphagnum moss, or peat. This material should be kept moist, but the overall environment should not be wet.

Tiger salamanders produce a great deal of waste; be prepared to change out the substrate often.

Continue to provide hiding spots for the salamanders, and vary the tank arrangement to facilitate cleaning and to keep the creatures interested in their environment.

Always supply a dish of water filled at a depth of 1-2 inches / 2.54-5.08 cm. Tiger salamanders enjoy soaking in water. Use dechlorinated water, and keep the supply in the dish fresh.

For adults the temperature range of 65 F - 70 F / 18 C - 21 C is still appropriate, but don't let the tank get warmer than 72 F / 22 C.

There is no need to use UV lighting with tiger salamanders, but it is important to keep them on a regular 12-hour rotation of light and dark.

For convenience sake, consider using a light with a timer. Programmable digital timers for use with reptile and amphibian terraria cost $20-$30 / £13-£19.

Diet and Feeding

To feed larval Tiger Salamanders use Daphnia (water fleas), brine shrimp, worms, and appropriately sized fish and insects.

Adults should be offered crickets, worms (mealworms, whiteworms, tubifex worms), and pinkie mice (immature mice sold in pet stores as pet food) as occasional treats.

Use a calcium supplement and dust the salamander's food daily. Use a vitamin and mineral power supplement one or two times a week.

It is best to feed the animals at night. The animals will be agreeable to "hand" feeding if you use tweezers. If you use crickets, remove any uneaten animals since they can bite your pet.

Tiger salamanders are beggars, which leads to chronic overfeeding and obesity. Don't let this cycle get started.

Sensitivity to Handling

Tiger salamanders should be handled as little as possible due to the extreme sensitivity of their skin. If you must handle your pet, be sure all residues have been washed from your hands with soap. Rinse well, and be extremely gentle.

Use a "scooping" motion and posture to pick up the tiger salamander and make sure that you full support the animal's body. Some experts recommend using latex gloves.

Notes on Health

Tiger salamanders are subject to the same health conditions as axolotls. The information contained in the chapter of this book on health will apply equally to these creatures. The conditions to which tiger salamanders are most prone include:

- Gas Bubble Disease (marked by bloating and bubbles under the creature's skin)
- Metabolic Bone Disease (which often leads to paralysis in tiger salamanders)
- Bacterial and fungal infections

Appendix 1 - Overview of Tiger Salamanders

The warning signs of ill health and disease in a tiger salamander include:

- changes in weight
- labored or rapid breathing
- skin lesions or mucous like discharges
- lethargic behavior
- bloating
- cloudy and dull eyes
- lack of coordination and poor balance

If your tiger salamander is healthy, it will eat regularly, maintain a normal weight, and have healthy skin and clear, bright eyes.

Breeding Tiger Salamanders

Most casual enthusiasts don't try to breed this species, leaving the task to professional reptile keepers. In order to be successful, at least 2 males and 3-4 females must be housed in a 40 gallon / 151.4 liter tank.

If you are interested in experiencing the animal's complete life cycle, it is not necessary to breed tiger salamanders to do so. They are frequently sold in their larval state, allowing hobbyists to play witness to the metamorphosis into adulthood.

It is important to understand that during and after the metamorphosis, the salamander's habitat will require alteration. You will need to watch your larval pet closely to be prepared to help the animal make a safe and healthy transition to adulthood.

Housing Multiple Species

Just as axolotls should only be housed with other axolotls, tiger salamanders must not be kept with any other species.

You certainly cannot let axolotls and tiger salamanders live together. Axolotls remain aquatic creatures for their entire lives. Tiger salamanders typically go through metamorphosis and become land-dwelling animals.

Appendix 1 - Overview of Tiger Salamanders

Relevant Websites

National Geographic Information on Axolotls
http://animals.nationalgeographic.com/animals/amphibians /axolotl/

Website Dedicated to Axolotl Information
http://www.axolotl.org/

Discussion Forum on Newts and Salamanders
http://www.caudata.org/forum/f46-beginner-newt-salamander-axolotl-help-topics/f48-axolotls-ambystoma-mexicanum/f57-axolotl-general-discussion/73932-playing-your-axolotl.html

Information on Axolotl Care
http://www.theaxolotl.net/

Learn how to care for an axolotl. Including guides on housing, breeding, feeding and more!
http://www.axolotlonline.com/

Miracle Healer: Scientists Attempt to Crack Secret Code of the Axolotl
http://www.spiegel.de/international/zeitgeist/miracle-healer-scientists-attempt-to-crack-secret-code-of-the-axolotl-a-732283.html

Relevant Websites

Frequently Asked Questions

Although it's recommend that you read the text in full to completely understand how to care for your axolotl, these are some of the questions most frequently asked about these interesting creatures.

Can I keep axolotls outside in a pond?

If the pond doesn't freeze solid during the cold months, and if the summer and fall temperatures stay in a range of 50-75 F / 10-24 C axolotls should do fine in a pond, but you will probably still need to feed them.

Can axolotls live in an aquarium with fish?

Regardless of temperament or species, tank mates for axolotls just aren't a good idea. If the fish are aggressive, they'll go after the axolotl's feathery gills. Other salamanders or newts may do the same thing. If, however, the axolotl is bigger than anything else living in the tank, "anything else" will be on the axolotl's dinner menu. Basically, anything that moves and that is smaller is fair game for an axolotl.

Aren't axolotls endangered?

Wild axolotls are listed as endangered, but those that are used in medical research and that are kept as pets are bred in captivity. Some countries do have specific regulations about owning amphibians. In Australia, for instance, the axolotl is the only non-native salamander that is allowed to be kept as a pet.

Can axolotls be kept with other axolotls?

Axolotls will live together quite well, but do be aware that when they are under 4 inches (10 cm), they will show some aggression and nipping if they don't have enough space. This kind of behavior is not a problem with adults.

Since it is so difficult to distinguish males from females, don't be surprised if you wind up with eggs. (See the chapter on breeding for tips on how to handle this situation.)

My axolotl is moving up and down the tank and periodically crashing into the glass. What's going on?

Rapid swimming and crashing into the glass is an indication that your axolotl has been frightened. Often this species mistakes a sudden movement in the room or even just the light coming on quickly as the presence of a predator. Basically the salamander is just trying to get away. Provide your pet with a hiding place so it can feel secure and find some place to get more relaxed.

Watch the axolotl's behavior closely. If it is not only crashing into the glass but thrashing as if it's trying to shake something off its body, it may be suffering from a skin irritation or parasites.

Should I use lighting in my axolotl's tank?

It's perfectly fine to use a typical aquarium light so long as the water does not become overheated. It's best to stay away from halogen bulbs. If you are going to use a light for aesthetic purposes, make sure your pet has some place to hide. If it's really showing signs of stress, lower the light's intensity.

I just caught my axolotl eating gravel. Should I be worried?

Normally axolotls have no difficulty passing gravel, but if they eat it in quantity, it can kill them. For your own peace of mind, put your pet on a bare tank bottom for a couple of weeks so you'll know for sure. If the gravel does become lodged, there's not a lot you can do.

Just watch the axolotl and consider changing the substrate or using none at all. If the animal does become blocked from the ingest gravel, the axolotl will likely float due to the build up of gas in its system.

Lower the water level in that event because the floating will only stress the creature more. If the salamander is still eating, that's a good sign.

What is the ideal temperature for an axolotl?

Strive for a temperature range of 50-68 F (10-20 C). Axolotls are cold water animals. You can't keep them at the same temperature levels as tropical fish. If the water gets over 77 F (25 C), the stress will kill your pet.

It looks like there's something sort of white and stringy growing on my axolotl. What's up with that?

If you begin to see white growths on your axolotl, the water temperature may be too high. What you are seeing is fungus, which is, in itself, harmless, but is an indicator of an unhealthy state for your pet. Be especially concerned if your axolotl isn't eating.

Gently bath your pet in mildly salty water for 10 minutes once or twice a day. (Go for about 2-3 teaspoons per two pints.) This should be enough to kill the fungus, but you must fix the water temperature and quality to remove the source of the stress.

I think my axolotl's gills are shrinking. Why would that happen?

It's possible there's not enough oxygen in the water. If your pet is going to the surface to "gulp" air that's not normal behavior. Test the water for high levels of ammonia. If you're not using a filter, you need to start.

Unless there are other signs of sickness, like mucous or cottony looking growths on the skin, improving the water quality should return your pet's gills to normal.

It looks like my axolotl's skin is getting flaky. What should I do?

At any sign of potential illness, always check water quality first. Examine your pet closely and look for blister-like lesions around the mouth. Immediately test the water for ammonia levels and make sure the water is near "neutral" for pH (7.0 to 7.4). In almost all cases, when water quality improves, so does your pet's health.

Is there any one reason why an axolotl won't eat?

Often the easiest explanation for why an axolotl won't eat is just that the temperature in the tank is too high. Generally bringing the water down to acceptable levels 50-68 F (10-20 C) will fix the situation. If that solution doesn't work, see the chapter on health for more suggestions.

I came in to find my axolotl floating. He's alive, but what can I do to help him?

First, lower the water level so the axolotl's feet can touch the bottom, but make sure he's still fully submerged. There is likely bacterial activity in the salamander's gut causing gas. As long as he's eating, he will pass the gas on his own. Make sure the water temperature is correct.

Why would I want an axolotl. Don't they just sit there?

While it is true that axolotls stay on the bottom of the tank, they are not completely passive pets. They will happily eat out of your hand, and they do learn to recognize their owners. When an axolotl is alert and engaged, it watches what's happening outside its tank. It may sit up to get your attention, or even put its "hand" on the side of the tank in greeting.

The primary reason people cite for keeping axolotls as pets is their uniqueness in comparison to a relatively low maintenance profile.

Additionally, if well cared for, these creatures can live as long as 15 years. With their feathery gills and whimsical half "smiles," it's much easier to get attached to an axolotl than you may realize.

Why are axolotls used in medical research?

The fact that these animals stay in their immature state for life and never actually grow into salamanders makes them unique. They have incredible abilities to regenerate lost limbs, and even parts of their brain and spinal cord.

In lab experiments, scientists have transplanted organs from one axolotl to another with no resulting rejection on the part of the recipient. Additionally, these amazing creatures are 1000 times more resistant to cancer than humans.

The potential for axolotl research is huge, offering cures for diseases, treatments for burn patients, anti-aging solutions – even help for paralyzed patients.

How long does it take an axolotl to grow a new limb?

The rate of regeneration for axolotls that have lost limbs varies by age of the animal, temperature of the water, and quality of the water among other factors.

Younger animals show faster rates of regeneration, often growing a new limb in as little as a month. In older animals, the process can take several months.

One of the most fascinating things about limb regeneration in axolotls is that every new limb is absolutely perfect. There is no way to distinguish it from the rest of the body, and no sign of scar tissue whatsoever.

Amazingly, under laboratory conditions, one axolotl has shown the ability to regenerate body parts literally hundreds of times with no deviation from this biological standard of perfection.

Frequently Asked Questions

Glossary

A

acidity - The pH measurement judges the amount of acidity in water. It is an important measurement, but in terms of fiddler crab care, not as important as how much ammonia the water contains.

air pump - An air pump is a device used by aquarists to ensure that the water in their tank is properly oxygenated to support life.

alkalinity - The measure of water's alkalinity is a rating of its capacity to neutralize acid without causing pH levels to fall. In simplistic terms, the more acid that can be added to water before the pH begins to drop, the greater the alkalinity or "buffering" capacity of the water.

ambystoma - The term to describe the cup-like mouth of an axolotl. To feed, the creature opens its mouth and sucks in food, swallowing it whole, since axolotls do not have teeth, but only nubs capable of gripping food.

ammonia - This gaseous compound builds up in aquarium water as a consequence of the axolotl's waste and any decaying plant or food matter in the water. It is highly toxic to the axolotl and must be managed either by establishing the nitrogen cycle in the tank, or through frequent water changes. Testing for ammonia levels weekly is a must with this species.

Glossary

amphibian - These animals are vertebrates with cold blood that typically begin life in the water with gills, then develop legs and lungs, which allows them to emerge onto land to live. Axolotls never reaching this final stage of development. They have only rudimentary lungs, and spend their life in the water.

aquarist - Any person who owns and manages a home aquarium for pleasure.

aquarium - A self-contained glass or acrylic structure in which aquatic life forms are kept as pets. This includes fish and other animals dependent on a water-based environment, including axolotls.

C

carbonate hardness - An expression of the ability of water in your aquarium to absorb and neutralize acid.

carbon dioxide (CO2) - A colorless, odorless gas created by animal respiration. Its presence in an aquarium must be countered by the use of an air filter to oxygenate the water.

carnivore - An animal that eats meat as its primary food source. Axolotls are carnivores, and as adults, will eat either live or dead food. Juveniles will eat only live food.

chlorination - The process of adding chlorine to water as a purification agent to make it fit for human consumption.

Water used in aquariums must be de-chlorinated or the tank inhabitants may sicken and die.

cloacal - This is the cavity on an amphibian directly under the tail in an area referred to as the vent. It houses the reproductive organs, as well as the intestinal and urinary tracts.

cycling - The process of establishing the nitrogen cycle in a tank to create the presence of beneficial bacteria to convert toxic ammonia to nitrates. If this cycle is not appropriately cultivated, the ammonia will reach toxic and fatal levels in short order.

G

gills - The three pairs of breathing organs found on the sides of the axolotl's head that appear to be feathered or fluffy "branches."

H

hatchling - Immediately after hatching, young axolotls are referred to as "hatchlings." As they grow, they will become highly carnivorous and cannibalistic if not separated.

J

juvenile - Juvenile axolotls have reached the stage in life where their limbs are fully formed, but they have not yet reached sexual maturity. This final milestone of development typically does not occur until 18 months of age.

L

larva - The rudimentary stage of development in the axolotl's lifecycle when legs are not present.

N

neoteny - A state of existence also known as pedogenesis. Neotenous animals retains their juvenile or larval form for life, even after sexual maturity.

P

pedicalate - A mouth in which no true teeth are present, only nubs useful for holding food but not for cutting and biting.

poikilothermic - Animals that are cold blooded and require external sources of heat.

R

regeneration - The growth of new cells after an injury. The axolotl's ability to achieve this re-growth make it invaluable for medical research.

S

spermatophores - Male axolotls deposit these capsules, containing sperm, on the floor of the aquarium during mating.

substrate - Any base materials placed on the floor of the aquarium. For axolotls, a bare floor or flat pieces of slate work best, as the animals can swallow gravel and develop intestinal blockages.

T

territorial - Of or relating to a real or perceived sense of ownership of an area of the land, sea, or immediate environment. Fiddler crabs are highly territorial and can become aggressive in captivity if housed incorrectly.

V

vent - An opening on the underside of the axolotl under the tail where the sexual organs are located and where the animals waste products exit the body.

W

water quality - A term referring to the chemical composition of water at any given time.

Glossary

Selected Additional Reading

For anyone interested in the scientific role of axolotls in medical research, we are providing a sampling of the scholarly literature from the last decade as a jumping off point for broader reading on this topic.

Bachvarova, Rosemary F, Masi, Thomas, Drum, Matthew, Parker, Nathan, Mason, Ken, Patient, Roger, and Johnson, Andrew D. "Gene Expression in the Axolotl Germ Line: Axdazl, Axvh, Axoct-4, and Axkit." Developmental Dnamics 231, no. 4 (2004): 871-80.

Badawy, Gamal, and Reinecke, Manfred. "Ontogeny of the Vip System in the Gastro-intestinal Tract of the Axolotl, Ambystoma Mexicanum: Successive Appearance of Co-Existing Pacap and Nos." Anatomy and Embryology 206, no. 4 (2003): 319-25.

Bride, IG, Griffiths, RA, Melendez-Herrada, A, and McKay, JE. "Flying an Amphibian Flagship: Conservation of the Axolotl Ambystoma Mexicanum Through Nature Tourism At Lake Xochimilco, Mexico." International Zoo Yearbook 42, no. 1 (2008): 116-24.

Campbell, Leah J, Suárez-Castillo, Edna C, Ortiz-Zuazaga, Humberto, Knapp, Dunja, Tanaka, Elly M, and Crews, Craig M. "Gene Expression Profile of the Regeneration Epithelium During Axolotl Limb Regeneration." Developmental Dynamics 240, no. 7 (2011): 1826-40.

Selected Additional Reading

Cerny, Robert, Meulemans, Daniel, Berger, Jürgen, Wilsch-Bräuninger, Michaela, Kurth, Thomas, Bronner-Fraser, Marianne, and Epperlein, Hans-Henning. "Combined Intrinsic and Extrinsic Influences Pattern Cranial Neural Crest Migration and Pharyngeal Arch Morphogenesis in Axolotl." Developmental Biology 266, no. 2 (2004): 252-69.

Cosden, RS, Lattermann, C, Romine, S, Gao, J, Voss, SR, and MacLeod, JN. "Intrinsic Repair of Full-thickness Articular Cartilage Defects in the Axolotl Salamander." Osteoarthritis and Cartilage 19, no. 2 (2011): 200-05.

Dixon, James E, Allegrucci, Cinzia, Redwood, Catherine, Kump, Kevin, Bian, Yuhong, Chatfield, Jodie, Chen, Yi-Hsien, Sottile, Virginie, Voss, S Randal, and Alberio, Ramiro. "Axolotl Nanog Activity in Mouse Embryonic Stem Cells Demonstrates That Ground State Pluripotency is Conserved From Urodele Amphibians to Mammals." Development 137, no. 18 (2010): 2973-80.

Epperlein, Hans H, Vichev, Konstantin, Heidrich, Felix M, and Kurth, Thomas. "Bmp-4 and Noggin Signaling Modulate Dorsal Fin and Somite Development in the Axolotl Trunk." Developmental Dynamics 236, no. 9 (2007): 2464-74.

Ericsson, Rolf, Cerny, Robert, Falck, Pierre, and Olsson, Lennart. "Role of Cranial Neural Crest Cells in Visceral Arch Muscle Positioning and Morphogenesis in the Mexican Axolotl, Ambystoma Mexicanum." Developmental Dynamics 231, no. 2 (2004): 237-47.

Selected Additional Reading

Ericsson, Rolf, and Olsson, Lennart. "Patterns of Spatial and Temporal Visceral Arch Muscle Development in the Mexican Axolotl (ambystoma Mexicanum)." Journal of Morphology 261, no. 2 (2004): 131-40.

Fritzsch, Bernd, Gregory, Darin, and Rosa-Molinar, Eduardo. "The Development of the Hindbrain Afferent Projections in the Axolotl: Evidence for Timing as a Specific Mechanism of Afferent Fiber Sorting." Zoology 108, no. 4 (2005): 297-306.

Gibbs, Melissa A, and Northcutt, R Glenn. "Retinoic Acid Repatterns Axolotl Lateral Line Receptors." International Journal of Developmental Biology 48, no. 1 (2004): 63-66.

Golub, Rachel, André, Sébastien, Hassanin, Alexandre, Affaticati, Pierre, Larijani, Mani, and Fellah, Julien S. "Early Expression of Two Tdt Isoforms in the Hematopoietic System of the Mexican Axolotl." Immunogenetics 56, no. 3 (2004): 204-13.

Gorsic, M, Majdic, G, and Komel, Radovan. "Identification of Differentially Expressed Genes in 4-day Axolotl Limb Blastema By Suppression Subtractive Hybridization." Journal of Physiology and Biochemistry 64, no. 1 (2008): 37-50.

Hess, Katja, Steinbeisser, Herbert, Kurth, Thomas, and Epperlein, Hans-Henning. "Bone Morphogenetic Protein-4 and Noggin Signaling Regulates Pigment Cell Distribution in the Axolotl Trunk." Differentiation 76, no. 2 (2008): 206-18.

Huggins, P, Johnson, CK, Schoergendorfer, A, Putta, S, Bathke, AC, Stromberg, AJ, and Voss, SR. "Identification of Differentially Expressed Thyroid Hormone Responsive Genes From the Brain of the Mexican Axolotl (Ambystoma Mexicanum)." Comparative Biochemistry and Physiology Part C: Toxicology & Pharmacology 155, no. 1 (2012): 128-35.

Johnson, Andrew D, Crother, Brian, White, Mary E, Patient, Roger, Bachvarova, Rosemary F, Drum, Matthew, and Masi, Thomas. "Regulative Germ Cell Specification in Axolotl Embryos: a Primitive Trait Conserved in the Mammalian Lineage." Philosophical Transactions of the Royal Society of London. Series B: Biological Sciences 358, no. 1436 (2003): 1371-79.

Johnson, Andrew D, Crother, Brian, White, Mary E, Patient, Roger, Bachvarova, Rosemary F, Drum, Matthew, and Masi, Thomas. "Regulative Germ Cell Specification in Axolotl Embryos: a Primitive Trait Conserved in the Mammalian Lineage." Philosophical Transactions of the Royal Society of London. Series B: Biological Sciences 358, no. 1436 (2003): 1371-79.

Kragl, Martin, Knapp, Dunja, Nacu, Eugen, Khattak, Shahryar, Maden, Malcolm, Epperlein, Hans Henning, and Tanaka, Elly M. "Cells Keep a Memory of Their Tissue

Selected Additional Reading

Origin During Axolotl Limb Regeneration." Nature 460, no. 7251 (2009): 60-65.

Kragl, Martin, Knapp, Dunja, Nacu, Eugen, Khattak, Shahryar, Maden, Malcolm, Epperlein, Hans Henning, and Tanaka, Elly M. "Cells Keep a Memory of Their Tissue Origin During Axolotl Limb Regeneration." Nature 460, no. 7251 (2009): 60-65.

Mansour, N, Lahnsteiner, F, and Patzner, RA. "Collection of Gametes From Live Axolotl, Ambystoma Mexicanum, and Standardization of in Vitro Fertilization." Theriogenology 75, no. 2 (2011): 354-61.

Mchedlishvili, Levan, Epperlein, Hans H, Telzerow, Anja, and Tanaka, Elly M. "A Clonal Analysis of Neural Progenitors During Axolotl Spinal Cord Regeneration Reveals Evidence for Both Spatially Restricted and Multipotent Progenitors." Development 134, no. 11 (2007): 2083-93.

Nye, Holly LD, Cameron, Jo Ann, Chernoff, Ellen AG, and Stocum, David L. "Extending the Table of Stages of Normal Development of the Axolotl: Limb Development." Developmental Dynamics 226, no. 3 (2003): 555-60.

Page, Robert B, Voss, Stephen R, Samuels, Amy K, Smith, Jeramiah J, Putta, Srikrishna, and Beachy, Christopher K. "Effect of Thyroid Hormone Concentration on the Transcriptional Response Underlying Induced

Metamorphosis in the Mexican Axolotl (ambystoma)."
BMC Genomics 9, no. 1 (2008): 78.

Piekarski, Nadine, and Olsson, Lennart. "A Somitic
Contribution to the Pectoral Girdle in the Axolotl Revealed
By Long-term Fate Mapping." Evolution & Development
13, no. 1 (2011): 47-57.

Rao, Nandini, Jhamb, Deepali, Milner, Derek, Li, Bingbing,
Song, Fengyu, Wang, Mu, Voss, S Randal, Palakal, Mathew,
King, Michael, and Saranjami, Behnaz. "Proteomic Analysis
of Blastema Formation in Regenerating Axolotl Limbs."
BMC Biology 7, no. 1 (2009): 83.

Safi, Rachid, Bertrand, Stéphanie, Marchand, Oriane,
Duffraisse, Marilyne, de Luze, Amaury, Vanacker, Jean-
Marc, Maraninchi, Marie, Margotat, Alain, Demeneix,
Barbara, and Laudet, Vincent. "The Axolotl (ambystoma
Mexicanum), a Neotenic Amphibian, Expresses Functional
Thyroid Hormone Receptors." Endocrinology 145, no. 2
(2004): 760-72.

Sato, Kazuna, and Chernoff, Ellen AG. "The Short Toes
Mutation of the Axolotl." Development, Growth &
Differentiation 49, no. 6 (2007): 469-78.

Satoh, A, Graham, GMC, Bryant, SV, and Gardiner, DM.
"Neurotrophic Regulation of Epidermal Dedifferentiation
During Wound Healing and Limb Regeneration in the
Axolotl (Ambystoma Mexicanum)." Developmental
Biology 319, no. 2 (2008): 321-35.

Selected Additional Reading

Satoh, Akira, Bryant, Susan V, and Gardiner, David M. "Regulation of Dermal Fibroblast Dedifferentiation and Redifferentiation During Wound Healing and Limb Regeneration in the Axolotl." Development, Growth & Differentiation 50, no. 9 (2008): 743-54.

Satoh, Akira, Cummings, Gillian, Bryant, Susan V, and Gardiner, David M. "Neurotrophic Regulation of Fibroblast Dedifferentiation During Limb Skeletal Regeneration in the Axolotl (Ambystoma Mexicanum)." Developmental Biology 337, no. 2 (2010): 444-57.

Satoh, Akira, Gardiner, David M, Bryant, Susan V, and Endo, Tetsuya. "Nerve-induced Ectopic Limb Blastemas in the Axolotl Are Equivalent to Amputation-induced Blastemas." Developmental Biology 312, no. 1 (2007): 231-44.

Schnapp, Esther, Kragl, Martin, Rubin, Lee, and Tanaka, Elly M. "Hedgehog Signaling Controls Dorsoventral Patterning, Blastema Cell Proliferation and Cartilage Induction During Axolotl Tail Regeneration." Development 132, no. 14 (2005): 3243-53.

Shaikh, Nooreen, Gates, Phillip B, and Brockes, Jeremy P. "The Meis Homeoprotein Regulates the Axolotl Prod 1 Promoter During Limb Regeneration." Gene 484, no. 1 (2011): 69-74.

Smith, Jeramiah J, Kump, David Kevin, Walker, John A, Parichy, David M, and Voss, Stephen Randal. "A

Comprehensive Expressed Sequence Tag Linkage Map for Tiger Salamander and Mexican Axolotl: Enabling Gene Mapping and Comparative Genomics in Ambystoma." Genetics 171, no. 3 (2005): 1161-71.

Sobkow, Lidia, Epperlein, Hans-Henning, Herklotz, Stephan, Straube, Werner L, and Tanaka, Elly M. "A Germline Gfp Transgenic Axolotl and Its Use to Track Cell Fate: Dual Origin of the Fin Mesenchyme During Development and the Fate of Blood Cells During Regeneration." Developmental Biology 290, no. 2 (2006): 386-97.

Sobkow, Lidia, Epperlein, Hans-Henning, Herklotz, Stephan, Straube, Werner L, and Tanaka, Elly M. "A Germline Gfp Transgenic Axolotl and Its Use to Track Cell Fate: Dual Origin of the Fin Mesenchyme During Development and the Fate of Blood Cells During Regeneration." Developmental Biology 290, no. 2 (2006): 386-97.

Stéphane, Roy, and Mathieu, Lévesque. "Limb Regeneration in Axolotl: is it Superhealing?" The Scientific World Journal 6 (2006): 12-25.

Thomas, Anish, Rajan, Sudarsan, Thurston, Harold L, Masineni, Sreeharsha N, Dube, Preeti, Bose, Abhishek, Muthu, Vasundhara, Dube, Syamalima, Wieczorek, David F, and Poiesz, Bernard J. "Expression of a Novel Tropomyosin Isoform in Axolotl Heart and Skeletal

Muscle." Journal of Cellular Biochemistry 110, no. 4 (2010): 875-81.

Thurston, Harold L, Prayaga, Sastry, Thomas, Anish, Guharoy, Victor, Dube, Syamalima, Poiesz, Bernard J, and Dube, Dipak K. "Expression of Nkx2. 5 in Wild Type, Cardiac Mutant, and Thyroxine-induced Metamorphosed Hearts of the Mexican Axolotl." Cardiovascular Toxicology 9, no. 1 (2009): 13-20.

Valiente, Elsa, Tovar, Armando, González, Homán, Eslava-Sandoval, Dionisio, and Zambrano, Luis. "Creating Refuges for the Axolotl (ambystoma Mexicanum)." Ecological Restoration 28, no. 3 (2010): 257-59.

Whited, Jessica L, Lehoczky, Jessica A, and Tabin, Clifford J. "Inducible Genetic System for the Axolotl." Proceedings of the National Academy of Sciences 109, no. 34 (2012): 13662-67.

Zhang, C, Pietras, KM, Sferrazza, GF, Jia, P, Athauda, G, Rueda-de-Leon, E, Maier, JA, Dube, DK, Lemanski, SL, and Lemanski, LF. "Molecular and Immunohistochemical Analyses of Cardiac Troponin T During Cardiac Development in the Mexican Axolotl, Ambystoma Mexicanum." Journal of Cellular Biochemistry 100, no. 1 (2007): 1-15.

Selected Additional Reading

Index

Index

freshwater, 1, 40

gills, 15, 16, 17, 21, 22, 40, 61, 64, 66, 70, 71, 91, 105, 108, 110, 113, 114

intestinal blockages, 37

iodine, 14

iridophores, 21

larval, 14

leucistic, 22

lungs, 15, 17, 24

medical research, 14, 23, 81, 86, 89, 91, 105, 110, 115, 118

melanoid, 21

Mexican Walking Fish, 1, 13

Mexico, 1, 13

mouth, 1, 23

neotenous, 14, 15

pH, 39, 40, 41, 43, 60, 109

piebald, 20, 22

plants, 36, 37, 56, 74

pluripotentiality, 84

pump, 36, 45

refractometer, 40

Regenerated nerves, 83

retired, 89, 90

salamander, 1, 3, 13, 14, 103, 106, 107, 109

salinity of water, 40

secondary tank, 60, 75

sexual maturity, 18, 114, 115

spawning, 74

specific gravity, 40

spermatophores, 74, 75

spinal cord, 91

tanks, 34

temperature fluctuations, 16, 74

thermometer, 35

thyroxine, 14, 15

tiger salamander, 93, 94, 95, 96, 99, 100

toxic, 17, 37, 38, 41, 51, 53, 60, 70, 112, 114

transplants, 81

veterinarian, 24, 33, 68, 72

Index

Index

Made in the USA
Las Vegas, NV
17 November 2022

59523746R00075